Gnosis of the Mind

By
G. R. S. Mead

Copyright © 2020 Lamp of Trismegistus. All rights reserved. No part of this publication may be reproduced or transmitted in any form or by any means, electronic or mechanical, including photocopying, recording, or by any information storage and retrieval system, without permission in writing from Lamp of Trismegistus. Reviewers may quote brief passages.

ISBN: 978-1-63118-408-6

Esoteric Classics

Other Books in this Series and Related Titles

The Hymn of Jesus by G. R. S. Mead (978-1-63118-492-5)

Buddhist Psalms by Shinran (978-1-63118-465-9)

Confessions of an English Opium-Eater by T De Quincey (978-1-63118-485-7)

Qabbalistic Teachings and the Tree of Life by M P Hall (978-1-63118-482-6)

Rosicrucian Rules, Secret Signs, Codes and Symbols by various (978-1-63118-488-8)

The Sepher Yetzirah and the Qabalah by M P Hall (978-1-63118-481-9)

Fortune-Telling with Dice by Astra Cielo (978-1-63118-466-6)

The Janeites, The Man Who Would Be King and Other Stories of Freemasonry by Rudyard Kipling (978-1-63118-480-2)

Crystal Vision Through Crystal Gazing by Achad (978-1-63118-455-0)

Psalms of Solomon by King Solomon (978-1-63118-439-0)

The Path of Light: A Manual of Maha-Yana Buddhism (978-1-63118-471-0)

The Book of the Watchers by Enoch (978-1-63118-416-1)

Freemasonry and the Egyptian Mysteries by C W Leadbeater (978-1-63118-456-7)

The Mysteries of Freemasonry & the Druids by M P Hall &c (978-1-63118-444-4)

Magical Essays and Instructions by Florence Farr (978-1-63118-418-5)

Arcane Formulas or Mental Alchemy by W W Atkinson (978-1-63118-459-8)

The Machinery of the Mind by Dion Fortune (978-1-63118-451-2)

The Gospel of the Nativity of Mary by St. Matthew (978-1-63118-448-2)

A Collection of Fiction and Essays by Occult Writers on Supernatural, Metaphysical and Esoteric Subjects by various (978-1-63118-712-4)

The Leadbeater Reader: A Selection of Occult Essays (978-1-63118-483-3)

Audio versions are also available on Audible, Amazon and Apple

Table of Contents

Introduction…7

Gnosis of the Mind…9

INTRODUCTION

The word "esoteric" can be difficult to define. Esotericism in general can be seen less as a system of beliefs and more as a category, which encompasses numerous, different systems of beliefs. It's a bit of juxtaposition, since the word "esoteric" indicates something that few people know about, while the term itself broadly covers numerous philosophies, practices, areas of study and belief systems.

In a greater sense, Esotericism acts as a storehouse for secret knowledge, which is often considered ancient (by *tradition, if not by fact*), passed down from generation to generation, in private. At various times in history, simply possessing the knowledge of some of these subjects, was considered illegal and a jailable offence, if discovered. This usually included such general topics as Alchemy, Pharmacology, Qabalah, Hermeticism, Occultism, Ceremonial Magic, Astrology, Divination, Rosicrucianism and so on. Collectively, these areas of study were often referred to as the esoteric sciences.

Sometimes, the outer garment of a subject isn't esoteric, while what is hidden beneath it, is. As an example, Freemasonry isn't necessarily esoteric by nature (at *least not anymore)*, but certain signs, passwords and handshakes given to the candidate during their initiation, are in fact, esoteric, in the sense that they are hidden from the general public.

Today, in the twenty-first century, such topics are readily available at bookstores across the country, and numerous mainsteam publishers offer beginners guides and coffee-table volumes on many of these subjects, intended for mass appeal. Books like *"The Secret"* have turned previously arcane topics into household knowledge. All that being the case, however, it isn't to say that there still aren't buried secrets to uncover, ancient wisdom being ignored and forgotten mysteries to be explored. In fact, it is often that we are only able to further our own studies by standing on the shoulders of these disappearing giants.

Lamp of Trismegistus is doing its part to help preserve humanity's esoteric history by making some of these classics available to those students who are seeking to unearth the knowledge of these ancient colossi.

So, be sure to check other titles from our *Esoteric Classics* series, as well as our *Occult Fiction*, *Theosophical Classics*, *Foundations of Freemasonry Series*, *Supernatural Fiction*, *Paranormal Research Series*, *Studies in Buddhism* and our *Christian Apocrypha Series*. You can also download the audio versions of most of these titles from Amazon, Apple or Audible, for learning on the go.

THE GNOSIS OF THE MIND

For long I have been spending much of my time in a world of great beauty of thought and purity of feeling, created by the devotion and intelligence of one of the many theosophical fraternities of the ancient world. They called themselves disciples of Thrice-greatest Hermes, and sometimes spoke of their faith as the Religion of the Mind. They were prior to and contemporary with the origins and earliest centuries of Christianity, and they lived in Egypt.

What remains of their scriptures and what can be gleaned of their endeavour has recently been made accessible in the English tongue, in such fashion as I have been able to reproduce their thought and interpret it. The labour of many months is ended; the task of reproduction is accomplished, and the echoes of the Gnosis of Thrice-greatest Hermes are audible across the centuries for English ears in fuller volume than before, and I hope in greater clarity.

It is no small thing--this Gnosis of ten-thousand-times-great Hermes, as Zosimus in an ecstasy of enthusiasm calls Him; for it has as its foundation the Single Love of God, it endeavours to base itself upon the True Philosophy and Pure Science of Nature and of Man, and is indeed one of the fairest forms of the Gnosis of the Ages. It is replete with Wisdom (Theosophia) and Worship (Theosebeia) in harmony--the Religion of the Mind. It is in its beginning Religion, true devotion and piety and worship, based on the right activity and passivity of the Mind, and its end is the Gnosis of things-that-are and the Path of the Good that leads man unto God.

Do I claim too much for the Gnosis of Thrice-greatest Hermes? I do but echo what He teaches in His own words (or rather those of His disciples) turned into English speech. The claim made is for the Gnosis, not for the forms of its expression used by its learners and hearers. All these forms of expression, the many sermons, or sacred discourses, of the disciples of this Way, are but means to lead men towards the Gnosis; they are not the Gnosis itself. True, much that is set forth appears to me to be very beautifully expressed, and I have been delighted with many a thought and phrase that these nameless writers and thinkers of years long ago have handed down to us in the fair Greek tongue; all this however, is as a garment that hides the all-beautiful natural form and glory of the Truth.

What is of importance is that all these Theosophists of the Trismegistic tradition declare with one voice--a sweet voice, that carries with it conviction within, to the true knower in our inmost soul--that there is Gnosis and Certitude, full and inexhaustible, no matter how the doubting mind, opinion, the counterfeit mind, may weave its magic of contrary appearances about us.

Seeing, then, that I have now much in mind of what has been written of this Religion of the Mind, I would set down a few thoughts thereon as they occur to me, an impression or two that the contemplation of the beautiful sermons of the disciples of the Master-Mind has engraved upon my memory. And first of all I would say that I regard it as a great privilege to have been permitted by the Gods to be a hander-on in some small way of these fair things; for indeed it is a great privilege and high honour to be allowed in any fashion to forward the preparation for the unveiling of the beauties of the Gnosis in the hearts of one's fellows,--even in so insignificant a way as that of translating and commenting on that which has already been set forth by greater minds in greater beauty centuries ago. The feeling that so pleasant a task has been granted by the Providence of God as a respite on the way (to use a phrase of Plotinus'). And so, as in all sacred acts, we begin with praise and thankfulness to God, as Hermes teaches us.

But when is there (the disciple of the Master will interject) an act that is not sacred for one who is a "man" and not a "procession of Fate"? He who is coming unto himself, who from the unconscious and the dead is beginning to return to consciousness and rise into life, self-consecrates his every act for ever deeper realisation of the mystery of his divine nature; for now no longer is he an embryo within the womb, nourished in all things by the Mother-Soul, but a man-babe new born, breathing the freer spirit of the greater life, the cosmic airs of the Father-Mind. And so it is that every act and function of the body should be consecrated to the Soul and Mind; the traveller on this Way should pray unceasingly, by devoting his every act unto his God; thinking when eating: As this food nourishes the body, so may the Bread of Wisdom nourish the mind; or when bathing: As this water purifies the body, so may the Water of Life vivify the mind; or when freeing the body of impurities: As these impurities pass from the body, so may the refuse of opinion pass from the mind!

Not, however, that he should think that anything is in itself unclean or common, for all is of the divine substance and of mother-matter; this he already knows in his heart of hearts, but his lower members are not as yet knit together in right harmony; they are as yet awry, not centred in the perfect whole. He as yet sees things from only one point; he has not yet realised that *the* Point is everywhere, and that for everything there is a point of view whence it is true and right and beautiful and good. That all-embracing point of view is the one sense, all-sense, the common sense, the sense of the intelligence, in which the sensible and the intelligible are identical and not apart. It is the little mind, the mind in man, the fate-procession, that creates external duality; the Great Mind knows that the without and the within are twain in one, are self-conditioned complements, the one within the other and without the other at one and the same time.

In this Religion of the Mind there is no opposition of the heart and head. It is not a cult of intellect alone, it is not a cult of emotion alone; it is the Path of Devotion and Gnosis inseparably united, the true Sacred Marriage of Soul and Mind, of Life and Light, the ineffable union of God the Mother and God the Father in the Divine Man, the Logos, the Alone-Begotten of the Mystery of Mysteries, the All and One-- Ineffability and Effability eternally in simultaneous Act and Passion.

And if you should object to the word Mind as excluding other names of equal dignity, know that this also has been spoken of again and again by the disciples of Thrice-greatest Hermes.

He has no name, for He is the One of Many names, nay, He is the One of all names, for He is Name itself and all things else, and there is naught that is not He. Nor is He One alone, though He is the One and Only One, for He is All and Nothing, if such a thing as nothing there can be.

But we, because of our ignorance, call Him Mind, for Mind is that which knows, and ignorance seeks ever for its other self, and the other self of ignorance is Gnosis. And seeking Gnosis, whether it love or hate its own false view of what it seeks, ignorance is ever changing into some form of knowing, experiencing some novelty or other as it thinks, not knowing that it is experiencing itself. But Mind is not only that which knows, but also the object of all knowledge; for it knows itself alone, there being nothing else to know but Mind. It self-creates itself to know itself, and to know itself it must first not know itself. Mind thus makes ignorance and Gnosis, but is not either in itself. It is itself the Mystery that makes all mysteries in order that it may be self-initiate in all.

Thus we are taught that Mind, the Great Initiator, is Master of all masterhood, Master of all ignorance as well as knowledge. And so we find the Supreme addressing one of His Beloved Sons, one who has won the mastery of self, as "Soul of my Soul and Mind of My own Mind."

The Religion of the Mind is pre-eminently one of initiation, of perpetual perfectioning. The vista of possibility opened up to the mind's eye of the neophyte into these sacred rites transcends credibility. One asks oneself again and again: Can this be true? It seems too good to be true.

But how can it be "too good" (the Master smiles in reply) when the inevitable end of everything is the Perfection of perfection, The Good Itself?

It cannot be *too* good, for that which is too good is out of its own self; but with the Good there is neither too little nor too much, it is Perfection.

What then, we feebly ask, is imperfection? And in the Master-Presence we cannot but reply: It is the doubt "It is too good" that is the imperfection of our nature; we fear it cannot be for us, not knowing that the "little one" who catches some glimpse of the vista, the earnest of the Vision Glorious, sees not something without, but that which is within himself. It is all there potentially, the full Sonship of the Father. It *is* there and here and everywhere, for it is the nature of our very being.

The first glimpse of this Divine possibility is brought to the consciousness of the prepared disciple by the immediate Presence and Glory of the Master, according to the records of the followers of the Religion of the Mind. But who is the Master? Is He someone without us; is He some other one; is He some teacher who sets forth a formal instruction?

Not so. "This race," that is to say, he who is born in this natural way, "is never taught, but when the time is ripe, its memory is restored by God." It is not therefore some new thing; it is not the becoming of something or other; it is a return to the same, we become what we have ever been. The dream is ended and we wake to life.

And so in one of the marvellous descriptions of initiation handed on in the Trismegistic sermons, in which the disciple is reborn, or born in Mind, he is all amazed that his "father" and initiator here below should remain there before him just as he ever was in his familiar form, while the efficacious rite is perfected by his means. The "father" of this "son" is the link, the channel of the Gnosis; the true initiation is performed by the Great Initiator, the Mind.

And that this is so may be learned from another sermon, in which a disciple of a higher grade is initiated without any intermediate link; by himself, alone as far as any physical presence of another is concerned, he is embraced by the Great Presence and instructed in the mystery.

The office of the "father" is to bring the "son" to union with himself, so that he may be born out of ignorance into Gnosis, born in Mind, his Highest Self, and so become Son of the Father indeed.

What is most striking in the whole of the tradition of the Mind-doctrine is its impersonal nature. In this it stands out in sharp contrast with the popular Christianity and other saving cults contemporary with it. It is true that the sermons are set forth mostly in the form of instruction of teacher to pupil. We learn to love Hermes and Asclepius and Tat and Ammon, and become friends with all of them in turn; they seem to be living men, with well-marked characters. But they are not historical characters; they are types. There is an Ammon, a Tat, an Asclepius, and a Hermes, in each one of us, and that is why we learn to love them. The "holy four" are in the shrine of our hearts; but transcending all, embracing all, is the Shepherd of all men, the Love Divine that through the lips of our Hermes teaches us--as Asclepius or Tat or Ammon--as we have ears to hear the words of power, or eyes to see the gnostic splendour of the teaching.

Nay, more than this; such instruction, beautiful and true as it may be, is not the highest teaching of the Mind. They who are born in Mind, are taught by Mind by every act and every thought and every sensation. The Mind eternally instructs the man through body, soul and mind; for now the man begins to know through all of these, for he is changing from the little mind and soul and body that he was to the Great Body and Great Soul and Mind of the Great Man. He no longer seeks a teacher, for all things teach him, or rather the One Teacher teaches him through all. All that there is transforms itself for him into the nature of the Gnosis of the Good. No longer is he a hearer, but the Hearer; for he has ears on all sides to hear the voice of Nature, Spouse of the Divine, in everything that breathes and all that seems to have no life--the simultaneous winter and summer of the Lord.

No longer is he a seer, but the Seer; for he has eyes on all sides to see the beauty of the whole, and fairest things in things that are most foul.

No longer is he a doer, but the Doer; for all he does is consecrated to the Lord who dedicates Himself to acting in the man.

And so all of his senses and his energies are set on the Great Work of self-initiation in the Mysteries of God; his life becomes illumined by the glory of perpetual perfectioning, and he no longer thinks that he has ever been other than now he is. For memory is ever present with him, and the memory of the Mind is of the nature of eternity, which transcends all time and sees all past and future and all present in the instant that endures for evermore.

And what does the Religion of the Mind teach us of God, the universe and man? It teaches us many things of great solemnity and joyous presage; but one thing especially it seems to teach, and that is the impossibility of human speech to tell the mystery. For every man is but a letter in the language of the Gods; so that all that a man may write, no matter how well stocked his mind may be with systems of the world or of theology, or with the science of the human state, no matter how exactly he may reproduce his thought and trick it forth in fairest human language--all that he can express is but a single letter of his Word. The Words of God are written with the general purposed acts of men, and are not uttered by their individual spoken speech or penned with written words. The Words of

God are spoken by the energies of Nature, and are not written on the surfaces of things; the surfaces of things are scribbled over with the false appearances that men project from their unknowing minds.

How then can men describe the universe, except by their inscribing of themselves upon the fields of space? To describe the universe as it is they must become the universe, and then they will describe themselves; and to describe themselves they will be able to discover no better way than that in which the universe gives utterance to itself. It speaks perpetually the Language of the Gods, the Universal Tongue, for it is God for ever giving utterance unto Himself.

The Tongue of the Eternal is the Mind of God. It is by Mind, the Reason of His Self-subsistence, that He perpetually speaks forth all things.

Thus we learn that the Religion of the Mind is preeminently the Religion of the Logos, and throughout the whole of our Trismegistic tractates no name comes more frequently before us than the word Logos. For the Logos is the Word of God, not in the sense of a single Word, but the Word in the sense of the Universal Scripture of all worlds and of all men.

And so it is that Hermes is the Scribe of the Gods. Not that Hermes is one of the Gods who is a scribe for the rest, as though they could not write themselves; but Hermes is the Logos of God, and the Words he writes are Gods.

We men are letters of our Word or our God; for man has the glorious destiny before him, nay, the actuality even now in his universal nature, of being a God, a Divine Being, of the nature of Gnosis and Joy and Subsistence. That Word has written itself many times in the world, now one letter and now another; it spells itself in many ways, in sequences of lives of men, and of other lives as well.

And time will be when each and every God-Word, in its own proper turn, will sound forth in all its glory, not letter by letter, but the whole Word simultaneously on earth; and a Christ will be born and all Nature will rejoice, and the world of men will know or be ignorant according to the nature of the times and the manner of the utterance of the Word.

Such are some of the ideas aroused by some of the leading conceptions of the Religion of the Mind, or the Pure Philosophy, or Single Love, as the disciples of Thrice-greatest Hermes called their Theosophy some nineteen centuries ago.

The most general term, however, by which they named their science and philosophy and religion was Gnosis; it occurs in almost every sermon and excerpt and fragment of their literature which we possess. The doctrine and the discipline of Mind, the Feeder of men and Shepherd of man's soul, are summed up in that fairest word--Gnosis.

Let us then briefly consider the meaning of the name as the followers of this Way understood it. Gnosis is knowledge; but not discursive knowledge of the nature of the multifarious arts and sciences known in those days or in our own. On this "noise of words," these multifarious knowledges of the appearances of things and vain opinions, the followers of the True Science and Pure Philosophy looked with resignation; while those of them who were still probationers treated them with even less tolerance, declaring that they left such things to the "Greeks"; for "Egyptians," of course, nothing but Wisdom could suffice.

At any rate this is how one of the less instructed editors of one of the collections of our sermons phrases it. For him Egypt was the Sacred Land and the Egyptians the Chosen Race; while the Greeks were upstarts and shallow reasoners. The like-natured Jew of the period, on the other hand, called the body "Egypt," while Judæa was the Holy Land, and Israel the Chosen of God; and so the game went merrily on, as it does even unto this day.

But the real writers of the sermons knew otherwise. Gnosis for them was superior to all distinction of race; for the Gnostic was precisely he who was reborn, into *the* Race, the Race of true Wisdom-lovers, the Kinship of the Divine Fatherhood. Gnosis for them began with the Knowledge of Man, to be consummated at the end of the perfectioning by the Knowledge of God or Divine Wisdom.

This Knowledge was far other than the knowledge or science of the world. Not, however, that the latter was to be despised; for all things are true or untrue, according to our point of view. If our standpoint is firmly centered in the True, all things can be read in their true meaning; whereas if we wander in error, all things, even the truest, become misleading for us.

The Gnosis began, continued and ended in the knowledge of one's self, the reflection of the Knowledge of the One Self, the All Self. So that if we say that Gnosis was other than the science of the world, we do not mean that it excluded anything, but only that it regarded all human arts and sciences as insufficient, incomplete, imperfect.

Indeed it is quite evident on all hands that the writers of the Trismegistic tractates, in setting forth their intuitions of the things-that-are, and in expressing the living ideas that came to birth in their hearts and heads, made use of the philosophy and science and art of their day. It is, in very deed, one of the stories of their endeavour that they did so; for in so doing they brought the great truths of the inner life into contact with the thought of their age.

There is, however, always a danger in any such attempt; for in proportion as we involve the great intuitions of the soul and the apocalypses of the mind in the opinions of the day, we make the exposition of the mysteries depart from the nature of scripture and fall into the changing notions of the ephemeral. Human science is ever changing; and if we set forth such glimpses of the sure ideas and living verities of the Gnosis as we can obtain, in the ever-changing forms of evolving science, we may, indeed, do much to popularise our glimpse of the mysteries for our own time; but the days that are to come will accuse us of clothing the Beauty of the Truth in rags as compared with the fairer garments of their own improved opinions.

The documents that have been preserved from the *scriptoria* of the Trismegistic tradition are by many hands and the product of many minds. Sometimes they involve themselves so closely with the science of their day that the current opinion of the twentieth century will turn from them with a feeling of contemptuous superiority; on the other hand they not infrequently remain in the paths of clear reason, and offer us an unimpeded view of vistas of the Plain of Truth. But even when they hold most closely to the world-representations and man-knowledges of their own day they are not without interest; for it may be that in their notions of living nature--the very antipodes of our modern day opinions based on the dead surfaces of things--they may have been with regard to some things even nearer the truth than we are ourselves in this so boasted age of grace and enlightenment.

Be this as it may, there are many examples of clean and clear thinking in the *logoi* or sacred sermons, or discourses, or utterances, of the School; and one of the most attractive elements in the whole discipline is the fact that the pupil was encouraged to think and question. Reason was held in high honour; a right use of reason, or rather, let us say, right reason, and not its counterfeit, opinion, was the most precious instrument of knowledge of man and the cosmos, and the means of self-realisation into that Highest Good which, among many other names of sublime dignity, was known as the Good Mind or Reason (Logos) of God.

The whole theory of attainment was conditioned by the fact that man in body, soul and mind was a world in himself--a little world, it is true, so long as he is content to play the part of a "procession of Fate"; but his Destiny is greater than that Fate, or rather, let us say, his Unknowingness is Fate, his Awareness will be his Destiny. Man is a little world, little in the sense of personal, individual, separate; but a world for all that--a monad. And the destiny of man is that he should become the Monad of monads, or the Mind of God--the Cosmos itself, not only as perceived by the senses as all that is, both that which moves and moves not, which is the Great Body and Great Soul of things; but also as conceived by mind, as that Intelligible Greatness of all greatnesses, the Idea of all ideas, the Mind and Reason of God Himself, His own Self-created Son, Alone-begotten, the Beloved.

On this transcendent fact of facts is founded the whole discipline and method of the Gnosis of the Mind. The Mystery of mysteries is Man or Mind. But this naming of the Mystery should not be understood as excluding Soul and Body. Mind is the Person of persons, the Presence of all presences. Time, space, and causality are conditioned by the Mind. But this Mind, the True Man, is not the mind in bondage to causality, space and time. On the other hand, it is just this mind in bondage, this "procession of Fate," the "servant's form," which is the appearance that hides the potentiality of becoming the All, of becoming the Æon, the Presence,--that is, the Subsistence of all things present, at every moment of time, and point of space, and every instant cause-and-effect in the Bosom of Fate. It is true that in the region of opinion, body, soul and mind seem separate and apart; they are held by the man in separation as the fundamental categories of his existence; and truly so, for they are the conditions of *ex*-istence, of standing *out* of Being, that environment of incompleteness--the complement or fulfilment of which is *ec*-stasis, whereby the man goes forth from his limitations to unite himself with Himself, and so reaches that Satisfaction and Fulfilment, which our Gnostics call the PLEROMA when set over against the conception of space, and the Æon when set over against the idea of time, and the Good when contrasted with the notion of Fate.

But Being is the Three in One, Mind, Soul and Body--Light, Life and Substance, co-eternal together and co-equal.

It therefore follows that he who would be Gnostic, must not foolishly divorce within himself the mystery of the triple Partners, the Three Powers, or the Divine Triad. For him the object of his endeavour is to consummate the Sacred Marriage within himself, where Three must "marry" to create; that so he may be united to his Greatest Self and become at-one with God. Body, soul, and mind (or spirit, for in this Gnosis spirit is frequently a synonym of mind) must all work together in intimate union for righteousness.

The body of man must be regarded as a holy temple, a shrine of the Divine--the most marvellous House of God that exists, fairer far than the fairest temple raised with hands. For this natural temple which the Divine has wrought for the indwelling of His beloved sons, is a copy of the Great Image, the Temple of the Universe in which the Son of God, the Man, dwells.

Every atom of every group of atoms, every limb and joint and organ, is laid down according to the Divine Plan; the body is an image of the Great Seal, Heaven-and-Earth, male-female in one.

But how few know or even dream of the possibilities of this living temple of the Divine! We are sepulchres, tombs of the dead; for our bodies are half-atrophied, alive only to the things of Death, and dead to the things of Life.

The Gnosis of the Mind thus teaches us to let the Life flow into the dead channels of our corporeal nature, to invoke the Holy Breath of God to enliven the *substance* of our frames, that so the Divine Quickener may first bring to birth in us our divine complement, our other self, our long-lost spouse, and then we may ourselves with ungrudging love and fair wooing of her bring our true selves to birth, so becoming regenerate or reborn,--a trinity of Being, not a unit of vegetative existence, or a duality of man-animal nature, but the Perfect Triangle jewelled with all three sparks of perfected manhood.

It is very evident, then, that if the idea of this Gnosis be carried out logically, the hearer of this Mathesis must strive ever to become a doer of the Word, and so self-realise himself in every portion of his being. The object that he has in view is intensification of his whole nature. He does not parcel out his universe or himself into special compartments, but he strives ever to refund himself into ever more intimate union with himself--meaning by this his ever-present consciousness; for there is nothing really that he is not.

Indeed it is one of the pleasantest features of the Trismegistic Gnosis, or rather, one may say its chief characteristic, a characteristic which should specially endear it to our present age, that throughout it is eminently reasonable. It is ever encouraging the pupil to think and question and reason; I do not mean that it encourages criticism for the sake of pedantic carping, or questioning for the sake of idle curiosity, but that it is ever insisting on a right use of the purified reason, and the striving to clarify the mind and soul and body, so that they may become a crystal prism through which the One Ray of the Logos, the All-Brilliancy, as Philo calls it, many shine with unimpeded lustre in clean and clear colours according to the nature of the truth in manifestation.

And here we may attempt to compare, though not with any idea of contrasting to the disparagement of either, the greater simplicity of the Gnosis of the Mind with the dazzling multiplicity and endless immensities of the, perhaps for my readers, more familiar revelations of the Christianised Gnosis. They are two aspects of the same Mystery; but whereas the former is conditioned by the clear thinking of philosophic reason as set forth pre-eminently in the Logic of Plato, and refuses to sever its contact with the things-that-are "here" as well as "there," the latter soars into such transcendent heights of vision and apocalypsis, that it loses itself in ecstasies which cannot possibly be registered in the waking consciousness.

I, for my part, love to try to follow the seers of the Christian Gnosis, in their soaring and heaven-storming, love to plunge into the depths and greatness of their spiritual intuitions; yet it cannot but be admitted that this intoxication of the spirit is a great danger for any but the most balanced minds. Indeed, it is highly probable that such unrestrained outpourings of divine frenzy as we meet with in some of the Christian Gnostic Apocalypses, were never intended to be circulated except among those who had already proved themselves self-restrained in the fullest meaning of the term.

The Trismegistic sermons show us that such rapts and visions were also the privilege of "them who are in Gnosis"; but they did not circulate the revelations of such mysteries; and though they taught the disciple to dare all things in perhaps more daring terms than we find recorded in any other scripture, they again and again force him to bring all to the test of the practical reason, that so the vital substance received from above may be rightly digested by the pure mind and fitly used to nourish the nature below.

But as for us who are hearers of the Gnosis, of Theosophy, wherever it is to be found, it would be unwise to reject any experience of those who have gone before upon the Way. Whether we call it the Gnosis of the Mind with the followers of Thrice-greatest Hermes, or the Gnosis of the Truth as Marcus does, or by many another name given it by the Gnostics of that day, it matters little; the great fact is that there *is* Gnosis, and that men have touched her sacred robe and been healed of the vices of their souls; and the mother-vice of the soul is ignorance, as Hermes says. But this ignorance is not ignorance of the arts and sciences and the rest, but ignorance of God; it is the true a-theism, the root-superstition of the human mind and heart,--the illusion that prevents a man realising the oneness of his true self with the Divine.

The dawning of this sacred conviction, the birth of this true faith, is the beginning of Gnosis; it is the Glad Tidings, the Gnosis of Joy, at whose shining Sorrow flees away. This is the Gospel, as Basilides the Gnostic conceived it, the Sun of Righteousness with healing in His wings; that is to say, the Father in the likeness of a dove--the Father of Light brooding over the sacred vessel, or divine chalice, or cup, the awakened spiritual nature of the new-born son.

This is the true baptism, and also the first miracle, as in the Gnosis of the Fourth Gospel, when the water of the watery spheres is turned into the wine of the spirit at the "first marriage."

But perhaps my readers will say: But this is the Christian Gnosis and not the Gnosis of the Mind! My dear friends (if you will permit me, I would reply), there is no Christian Gnosis and Trismegistic Gnosis; there is but one Gnosis. If that Gnosis was for certain purposes either associated with the name and mystic person of the Great Teacher known as Jesus of Nazareth, or handed on under the typical personality of Great Hermes, it is not for us to keep the two streams apart in heart and head in water-tight compartments. The two traditions mutually interpret and complete one another. They are contemporaneous; they are both part and parcel of the same Economy. Read the fragments of these two forgotten faiths, or rather the fragments of the two manifestations of this forgotten faith, and you will see for yourselves.

But again, some one may say (as a matter of fact not a few have already said): What do we want with a forgotten faith, fragmentary or otherwise? We are living in the twentieth century; we do not want to return to the modes of thought of two thousand years ago; we can create a new Gnosis that will interpret the facts of present-day science and philosophy and religion.

I too await the dawn of that New Age; but I doubt that the Gnosis of the New Age will be new. Certainly it will be set forth in new forms, for the forms can be infinite. The Gnosis itself is not conditioned by space and time; it is we who are conditioned by these modes of manifestation. He who is reborn into the Gnosis becomes, as I have heard, the Lord of time and space, and passes from man into the state of Superman and Christ, or Daimon and God, as a Hermes would have phrased it two thousand years ago, or of Bodhisattva and Buddha, as it was phrased five hundred years before that.

Indeed, if I believe rightly, the very essence of the Gnosis is the faith that man can transcend the limits of the duality that makes him man, and become a consciously divine being. The problem he has to solve is the problem of his day, the transcending of his present limitations. The way to do so is not, I venture to submit, by exalting his present-day knowledge in science or philosophy or religion at the expense of the little he can learn of the imperfect tradition of the religion and philosophy and science of the past, handed on to us by the forgetfulness of a series of ignorant and careless generations. The feeding of our present-day vanity on the husks from the feasts of other days is a poor diet for one who would be Gnostic. It is very true that, speaking generally, we do know more of physical observation, analysis and classfication, we do know more of the theory of knowledge, and many other things in the domain of the lower world of appearances; but do we know more of religion as a living experience than the great souls of the past; do we know more of the Gnosis than the Gnostics of other days? I doubt it.

We are beginning once more to turn our attention in the direction of the Greater Mysteries; the cycles of the Æon are, I believe, once more set in a configuration similar to the mode of the Time-Mind when such illumination is possible for numbers of souls, and not for stray individuals only. But the conditions of receiving that illumination are the same now as they have ever been; and one of the conditions is the power to rise superior to the opinions of the Hour into the Gnosis of the Eternal Æon.

It therefore follows, if I am right in my premises, that the illusion of all illusions which we must strive to transcend is that of the Lord of the Hour; it is just the general opinions and presuppositions and prejudices of our own day against which we must be on our watch with greatest vigilance. There are certain forms of knowledge, forms of religion, and forms of philosophy, that dominate every age and every hour; these forms are most potent, for they are alive with the faith of millions; and therefore it follows that it may be we shall find less difficulty, in our endeavour to pierce through the clouds of opinion to the living ideas beyond, if we study forms that are no longer charged with the passions of mankind,--with that storage of the hopes and fears of incarnated minds, the shock of which few are strong enough to withstand. It may thus be that the forms of the Gnosis of the past may be read more dispassionately and seen through more clearly.

However this may be, it would be manifestly absurd to go back to the past and simply pour ourselves once more into these ancient forms; this would be death and a mental and spiritual "reincarnation" backwards, so to speak. It is precisely this absurdity which so many literalists attempt in theology, only to find themselves stranded among dead forms with the tide of the spiritual life far out.

On the other hand, there may be some who feel that in what has been said above, the artist and lover of the Beautiful in us risk to be sacrificed entirely to the Philistine. There is such a thing as scripture; there are such things as the best books. *Non refert quam multos sed quam bonos libros legas;* it is not the quantity but the quality of the books we read that is of importance. The Gnosis is enshrined in scripture, in bibles and not in books. And I doubt not that even to-day there are enough bible-lovers, in the wider sense of the word, among us to appreciate the beautiful and permanent in literature.

The Trismegistic sermons have a common language with the writers of the New Testament books, and they also use the language of Plato. They can, therefore, hardly be said to be out of date even as to their form; while as to their content, as far as their main ideas are concerned, I venture to say that they belong to the great books of the world, they are part of the world-scripture.

If, then, any would learn of the Gnosis of the Mind, they will not lose anything by reading what the disciples of this form of the Wisdom-Tradition have handed on to us. They may prefer more modern expositions, or they may find some other scripture of the past more suitable to their needs; but if they are lovers of comparative theosophy, and are persuaded that he who is acquainted with one mode of theosophy only does not know theosophy truly, even as he who is acquainted with one language only knows no language really, they may learn much by comparing the theosophy of the Hermes-Gnostics with the theosophy of the Christian Gnostics, or of the Buddhist or Brahmanical lovers of the Gnosis.

In conclusion, I would add a few quotations touching the Gnosis from the Trismegistic sermons; for, as Lactantius, the Church Father, tells us of the Holy Scribe who inspired these scriptures:

> "He wrote books, indeed many of them, treating of the Gnosis of things divine, in which he asserts the Greatness of the Highest and One and Only God" (iii., 233).

Yes, *He* wrote many books, whether we call Him "Hermes" or by any other of His many names. For as He says in another scripture of that Day of Sunshine, writing of the inner history of the Christ-Mystery, most probably before even there were as yet any Christian scriptures:

> "Wherefore, send me, O Father!
> Seals in my hands, I will descend;
> Through Æons universal will I make a Path;
> Through mysteries all I'll open up a Way!
> All Forms of Gods will I display;
> The Secrets of the Holy Path I will hand on,
> And call them Gnosis" (i., 192).

Yes, He wrote many books, many sermons and sacred discourses, entitled by many names, one of them called precisely: "An Introduction to the Gnosis of the Nature of All Things" (ii., 68).

Not that there is any precise beginning of the Gnosis or any definite introduction confined to any formal instruction; it may be presented in infinite modes to the learner and hearer, for it is like unto its Great Original.

And so we read:

> "For to the Good there is no other shore; It hath no bounds; It is without an end; and for Itself It is without beginning, too, though unto us It *seemeth* to have one--the Gnosis.

"Therefore to It Gnosis is no beginning; rather is it that Gnosis doth afford to *us* the first beginning of *Its being known*" (ii., 90).

And so again we find a Jewish mystic, who wrote just prior to the days of Paul, quoting from some scriptures of the Gnosis (in all probability from one of the lost sermons of our School) which sets forth the matter in still greater clarity in the striking aphorism:

"The beginning of Perfection is Gnosis of Man; but Gnosis of God is Perfect Perfection" (i., 178).

Thus Hermes in teaching his beloved son, the seeker, the suppliant and hearer, how to set his feet upon the path of self-realisation, points out the way in the wise and gentle words:

"Seek'st thou for God, thou seekest for the Beautiful. One is the Path that leadeth unto It--Devotion joined with Gnosis" (ii., 114).

And again he sets forth the boundary-marks of the Way of the Good Commandments in admirable instruction, saying:

"The Seeds of God, 'tis true, are few, but vast and fair and good--virtue and self-control, devotion. Devotion is God-Gnosis; and he who knoweth God, being filled with all good things, thinks godly thoughts and not thoughts like the many think.

"For this cause they who Gnostic are, please not the many, nor the many them. They are thought mad and laughed at; they're hated and despised, and sometimes even put to death....

"But he who is a devotee of God, will bear with all--once he has sensed the Gnosis. For such an one all things, e'en though they be for others bad, are for him good; deliberately he doth refer them all unto the Gnosis. And, thing most marvellous, 'tis he alone who maketh bad things good" (ii., 131).

The devotee of God is the Gnostic, and "they who are Gnostic" stand in the original as "they who are in Gnosis." It is of more than ordinary interest to compare this simple statement of fact addressed to "those in Gnosis" with the well-known words adapted from some early collection of "Logoi of the Lord" for the comfort of "those in Faith." What the Sayings preserved by the first and third evangelists may have been in their original form, we do not know, though any day the Oxhyrhynchus "rubbish-heaps" may yield us a clue. Some of these "Sayings of the Lord" which in their original form circulated in the inner communities, were, in the highest probability, subsequently adapted to the prophetical mood by a Christian evangelist prior to our first and third synoptists. Thus we find the writer of our First Gospel handing on one of these Sayings as:

> "Blessed are ye when they shall revile you and persecute you and shall say all manner of evil against you, lying, for My sake."

Here the "lying" is evidently the gloss of some scrupulous scribe who knew there were some things that could be said against them justly; whereas the third evangelist keeps closer to his original, writings:

> "Blessed are ye when *men* shall hate you, and when they shall separate you forth (from them), and revile you, and cast out your name as evil, for the sake of the Son of *the Man*."

But even so there still seems to be a blend of two traditions before the Saying reached the hands of our third evangelist. The antithesis between "men" and "Son of the Man" is familiar to us in our Trismegistic sermons, and would be understood by all who knew of the "Myth of Man in the Mysteries" (i., 139-198); it is clearly to be distinguished from the "My sake" of the first evangelist. Whereas the separating forth and the casting forth of the name as evil are, I believe, to be understood as expulsion of members of a community and the removal of their names from the list of the brethren.

But to return to the Gnosis. Devotion is God-Gnosis. True Piety is "nothing else than the Gnosis of God"--as Lactantius, quoting Hermes, phrases it in Latin (ii., 243). This piety, however, is something other than pious exercise and the practice of devotional worship; it leads unto "the complete or all-perfect contemplation," and embraces the "learning of the things-that-are, the contemplating of their nature and the knowing God"; or, in other words, the "being taught the nature of the all and the Supreme Vision" (ii., 264). And that Supreme Vision, if I understand aright, is no rapt into regions beyond the sky, but a Seeing of the Good in everything. For the Master of this Way teaches his disciple concerning the Gnosis of the Good, that is the Gnosis of God, saying:

> "For only then wilt thou upon It gaze when thou canst say no word concerning It. For Gnosis of the Good is holy silence and a giving holiday to every sense." It is the gaining of the "all sense," the "common sense," the "sense of the intelligence."

> "For neither can he who perceiveth It, perceive aught else, nor he who gazeth on It, gaze on aught else; nor hear aught else. . . .

> "And shining then all round his mind, It shines through his whole soul, and draws it out of body, transforming all of him to essence.

> "For it is possible, my son, that a man's soul should be made like to God, e'en while it still is in a body, if it doth contemplate the Beauty of the Good" (ii., 144).

This is the "deification" or "apotheosis" of a man; he becomes like unto God, in that he becomes a God. The Beauty of the Good is the Cosmic Order; and the mode of meditation was that of self-realisation whereby the soul is brought into sympathy with the Cosmic Soul.

And so speaking of such a soul, of one gnostic in true piety, Hermes writes:

> "But on the pious soul the Mind doth mount and guide it to the Gnosis' Light. And such a soul doth never tire in songs of praise to God and pouring blessing on all men, and doing good in word and deed to all, in imitation of its Sire" (ii., 155).

And so again in the outer preaching, in warning the multitude against the "fierce flood" of ignorance, the missionary of the Gnosis and evangelist of Salvation exhorts them, saying:

> "Be then not carried off by the fierce flood, but using the shore-current, ye who can, make for Salvation's port, and, harbouring there, seek ye for one to take you by the hand and lead you unto Gnosis' Gates.
>
> "Where shines clear Light, of every darkness clean, where not a single soul is drunk, but sober all they gaze with their hearts' eyes on Him who willeth to be seen.
>
> "No ear can hear Him, nor can eye see Him, nor tongue speak of Him, but only mind and heart" (ii., 121).

And from this preaching we learn the very interesting fact that there was some great association that the Gnostic evangelist regarded as Salvation's port, a harbour of refuge for many; but even when safe within the quiet of the discipline that could calm the waves of the fierce flood of passion and ignorance, there was still a further adventure for the soul before the Light of the New Day dawned. A guide who knew the Way to the Gates of the Spiritual Sun must be found, one who was "in Gnosis" and not only "in Faith."

For faith is conditioned upon feeling, upon sense, and not knowledge; as Hermes says:

"But Gnosis is far different from sense. For sense is brought about by that which hath the mastery o'er us, while Gnosis is the end of science, and science is God's gift" (ii., 147).

It is true that a refuge can be found in the Harbour of Salvation by means of Faith; but Salvation itself is Gnosis.

"This is the sole Salvation for a man--God's Gnosis. This is the Way up to the Mount.

"By Him alone the soul becometh good, not whiles is good, whiles evil, but good out of necessity" (ii., 150).

And again He says:

"The virtue of the soul is Gnosis. For he who knows, he good and pious is, and still while on the earth Divine" (ii., 146).

For in this view of the mystery, in consonance with the teaching of the Buddha, and with Indian theosophy in general, "the soul's vice is ignorance." And so we find Gnosis heading the list of virtues--Gnosis, Joy, Self-control, Continence, Righteousness, Sharing-with-all, Truth; a septenary consummated in the divine triad of Life, Light and the Good (ii., 246). For Gnosis is that which doth distribute life to all, and light to all, and good to all (ii., 296). And so the Master, in the spiritual theurgic rite at which he consecrates his beloved son to the holy life, declares:

"Gnosis of God hath come to us, and when this comes, my son, not-knowing is cast out.

"Gnosis of Joy hath come to us, and on its coming, son, sorrow will flee away to them who give it room" (ii., 225).

For it is by this "enformation according to Gnosis" that the man is made like unto the Great Man, the Good Mind or Reason of God. This Gnosis is not only Light and Life, the father-motherhood of God, but also Love. It is this Love of the Gnosis, of that which gives light and life to all, that urges on the disciple; it is the Breath of God Himself energizing in the heart, inspiring us. It is the Providence or Foresight of God, the Holy Spirit. And so in one of the sacred discourses, called "The Perfect Sermon," we read:

> "To them, sunk in fit silence reverently, their souls and minds pendent on Hermes' lips, thus Love Divine began to speak" (iii., 260).

To be Knowers we must be Lovers; we must have "the Single Love, the Love of wisdom-loving, which consists in Gnosis of Divinity alone--the practice of perpetual contemplation and of holy piety" (ii., 330).

Of such Lovers and such Gnostics we read:

> "But they who have received some portion of God's gift, these, son, if we judge by their deeds, have from Death's bonds won their release; for they embrace in their own mind all things, things on the earth, things in the heaven, and things above the heaven--if they be aught.
>
> "And having raised themselves so far they sight the Good; and having sighted It, they look upon their sojourn here as a mischance; and in disdain of all, both things in body and the bodiless, they speed their way unto that One and Only One.
>
> "This is, my son, the Gnosis of the Mind, vision of things Divine; God-knowledge is it, for the Mind is God's" (ii., 88).

Hard as it may be to leave the "things we have grown used to," the things habitual, it must be done if we are to enter into the Way of the Gnosis. But no new Path is this, no going forth into new lands (though it may have all the appearance of being so). The entrance on the Path of the Gnosis is a Going Home; it is a Return--a Turning-Back (a true Repentance of the whole nature). "We must turn ourselves back into the Old, Old Way" (ii., 98).

And for those who will thus "repent," there are promises and words of fair comfort spoken by the Mind Himself in the Gospel of the Gnosis called "The Shepherd of Men":

>"I, Mind, Myself am present with holy men and good, the pure and merciful, men who live piously.

>"To such my Presence doth become an aid, and straightway they gain Gnosis of all things, and win the Father's love by their pure lives, and give Him thanks, invoking on Him blessings and chanting hymns, intent on Him with ardent love" (ii., 14).

And to the truth of this, testimony is borne by one of those in Gnosis who had heard and had believed and had known, when he writes:

>"But I, with thanks and blessings unto the Father of the universal Powers, was freed, full of the Power He had poured into me, and full of what He'd taught me of the nature of the all and of the loftiest vision" (ii., 17).

And so he begins to preach to men "the Beauty of Devotion and of the Gnosis"; for he cannot refrain from uttering the Word, now that he has become a knower, a doer, and not a hearer only. He prays no longer for himself, but that he may be the means whereby the rest of human kind may come to Light and Life, saying:

> "Give ear to me who pray that I may ne'er of Gnosis fail, Gnosis which is our common being's nature; and fill me with Thy Power, and with this Grace of Thine, that I may give the Light to those in ignorance of the Race, my brethren and Thy sons" (ii., 20)

With these brief indications of the Gnosis of the Mind, drawn from a wealth of like noble teachings, we bring to an end the first volume of these "Echoes from the Gnosis," in the hope that there may be some who will turn to the fair originals, and "read, mark, learn and inwardly digest them."

www.ingramcontent.com/pod-product-compliance
Lightning Source LLC
LaVergne TN
LVHW041502070426
835507LV00009B/758